Anyone who has ever dreamed of being a magician will find out just how to go about it in this book.

In *Quick and Easy Magic Tricks* a master magician describes thirty-six of his favorite tricks for you—first as the audience sees them, and then as they are really performed. The magician suggests the kind of talk you might use to entertain your audience and distract their attention from your tricks during a performance. At the end of the book is a handy list of programs you might plan to give.

All of the tricks are surprisingly easy to learn. If you follow the ten golden rules, you will soon be able to put on The Greatest Magic Show on Earth!

QUICK AND EASY
MAGIC TRICKS

Gyles Brandreth
Illustrated by Mike Jackson

kidsbooks
Incorporated

KIDSBOOKS, INCORPORATED
7004 N. CALIFORNIA AVE.
CHICAGO, IL 60645

ISBN 0-942025-33-4

MANUFACTURED IN THE UNITED STATES OF AMERICA

Contents

Introduction

When I am cast away on my lonely desert island,
I shall certainly take with me:

17 coins
2 $1 bills
1 straw
1 dark-colored bottle
3 drinking glasses
1 tall-stemmed glass
1 plate
3 cups
2 envelopes
1 wand
1 bar of soap
1 writing pad
1 hat
1 blindfold
1 pair of scissors
1 piece of string
3 pieces of rope
1 tray
1 thimble
1 paper bag
1 paperback book
1 small piece of cork
1 table
1 stool
2 dice

1 scarf
1 bottle of water
2 bracelets
1 double-sided mirror
4 matchboxes
1 rubber band
1 spoon
a few handkerchiefs
a few pencils
some tape, sticky on both sides
some aluminum foil
several silk handkerchiefs
a pack of cards

Why? Simply because with all the items in this list I could perform all the tricks in this book—except those requiring an assistant, of course—and present the greatest magic show on earth!

Ten golden rules

Ten golden rules

1 Practice! Practice! Practice!

No one in the world can become a master magician overnight. It takes practice and lots of it. The more you practice, the better you will be. None of the tricks in this book require an incredible amount of practice, but they all need some. The One-star tricks are the easiest to perform and master. The Two-star tricks are not quite so easy, and the Three-star tricks will need to be worked on quite thoroughly.

At the beginning of the description of each trick you will find a list of the *Equipment* you need for the trick, followed by *The trick* itself. *The trick* shows you how the trick is "seen" from the audience's point of view. *The secret* tells you how the trick is done from the magician's point of view. Study this very, very carefully. Read *The secret* at least *twice* before you start to practice the trick and then practice the trick at least ten times before you show it to anyone. By then you should be really confident that you have mastered the trick.

The tricks involving sleight of hand — *Coining it!, Dollar power, The thimble vanishes, The wand and the handkerchief* — and the more spectacular tricks will need to be practiced a lot more often. If you try to perform them before you have really mastered them, you will only spoil them and show your audience that you are not a true magician.

2 Polish your patter

A magician's "patter" is what he or she says while performing a trick. The patter that goes with the description of each trick, in *The trick,* has been specially written just as if a real performance was taking place. You don't need to use the suggested patter, but you will probably find it handy while you are learning the trick. Of course you will want to develop your own style of patter. Keep it lively. Throw in as many good jokes as you like, particularly when you want to distract your audience!

3 Remember you're a showman

Above all, a magician is an entertainer. Never forget this fact. That's why your patter and your appearance are as important as your tricks. If you make your audience laugh, they will enjoy your magic that much more. And if you look the part — either because you're all dressed up as a wizard or because you're looking super magician-like — they will believe in your tricks more easily.

One other word about dressing up: a magician's hat is practically a must. It need not be a top hat, but you will need a hat with an inner lining. Check the descriptions for each trick. Your pockets and sleeves are part of the act too.

Be as confident as you can. Confidence will come with practice and experience. If you know you know your tricks, if you are sure all your props are in position, if you can see that you are looking the part, there is no need to be nervous. Nothing can go wrong. Don't rush your tricks, but at the same time keep the show moving.

4 Don't attempt the impossible

You might like to make rabbits appear out of hats and saw people in half, but only very experienced professional magicians with plenty of money can perform such elaborate tricks. One day, when you can afford the expensive equipment that more complicated tricks require, you can try throwing daggers and making a dozen doves appear out of nowhere. Meanwhile, stick to more straightforward magic. If properly performed, it can be as impressive to watch as the most elaborate tricks imaginable.

Most of the tricks in this book can be performed with props you find around the house. One calls for a special trick glass, that you can buy from a magic shop, and several require "magic" handkerchiefs. You can use ordinary handkerchiefs, but you will find it well worth spending your pocket money on some professional magician's "silks." These can be bought from any good magic shop. They come in all colors and are useful because they can be squeezed into tiny balls and hidden easily.

And remember: just because the One-star tricks are the easiest to master, it doesn't mean that they won't thrill your audience. Often the simplest trick is the one that baffles the audience most. All the tricks in this book have been or are being used by professional magicians all around the world.

5 Use your experience

As a magician, you will want to improve your performance all the time. The more shows you give, the better they will get; the more practice you give to a trick, the more polished it will become. With experience, you will probably want to change the way you present some of your tricks. Begin by doing them exactly as they are described in the book. Later, when you are really at home with them, you can change them to suit yourself.

Some tricks, you will find, lead to other tricks. For example, once you have learned how to "palm" an object (as you will in *Coining It!* on page 65), you will be able to use "palming" in all sorts of marvelous tricks of your own.

6 Use your audience

An audience likes to feel involved so, whenever you can, invite a member of the audience forward to help you. The audience will be less suspicious of your tricks also. Always use a member of the audience to blindfold you (unless, of course, you need to be able to peep under the blindfold!) but never use the same member of the audience twice during the same show. If you do, the rest of the audience will think you have an accomplice, or secret helper. You will be using an accomplice in some of your tricks, but you don't want the audience the know that fact. Sometimes you will be using an assistant, and, of course, you let the audience know.

7 Learn to mislead your audience

The more interesting your patter and the busier your hands, the less your audience will notice. You don't want your audience to see anything they're not supposed to see, so you must do all

you can to *misdirect* them at important moments in your performance. Remember that the audience will look where you look. Remember that they will look at anything you point to. Remember that they will look at anything that's moving.

8 Keep your wits about you

There are lots of card tricks described in this book, but the best card trick of all isn't included here at all! You will be amazed by how often, when you offer a pack of cards to a member of your audience and ask them to pick one, they accidentally let you catch sight of the card! It happens all the time. If you do happen to see the card, don't let on. Forget the trick you were going to perform and invent a new trick on the spot. It can be as clever as you like. It can *seem* impossible and, for once, it can *be* impossible. You know the secret card and that's all that counts.

9 Plan your show

A good magic show needs a splendid opening trick, a fantastic closing trick and lots of color and variety in between. It should never be too long. If you want some idea of what combination of tricks works well, take a look at *The Greatest Magic Show on Earth* on page 88.

10 Never! Never!

Never perform the same trick twice in the same show. If you do, your audience will begin to catch on to the way you do it. And *never, ever, EVER* tell anyone how any of your tricks are done!

One-star tricks

Silks from nowhere

Equipment: 2 silk handkerchiefs

The trick: My pockets are empty — and when I say *empty* I mean completely and utterly *empty*! Look: there's nothing in this one, and there's nothing in this one.

I've turned my pockets inside out to prove that they're empty, but if you all shout the mighty magic word *Shazzam!* something amazing may happen.

"Shazzam!"

No, my pockets are still empty. You'll have to shout louder than that.

"SHAZZAM!"

It's worked! Look at this beautiful red silk in my left pocket and this gorgeous blue one in my right pocket! They came from nowhere, thanks to you.

The secret: The silks didn't come from nowhere, of course — they came from inside your pockets. The audience didn't see where they were hidden when you turned your pockets inside out because there is what's called a "dead corner" in pants, or slacks, pockets where a small object

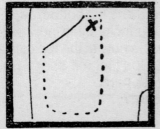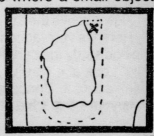

can be safely tucked and remain unseen even when the linings are turned out.

A magician's silk is a very useful piece of equipment to have. It looks just like a large silk handkerchief, but it is made of a material that can be squashed into a small shape very easily. Before beginning this trick, simply tuck two tightly rolled-up silks into the dead corners of your pants pockets. When you need to get the silks, put your hands in your pockets and work the silks out of the corners with your thumbs. Then produce them with a grand gesture!

Card sharp

Equipment: 1 pack of cards

The trick: To perform this trick I need the assistance of a member of the audience. Will you volunteer? Thank you very much, sir.

Now I would like you to take this pack of cards and cut it in two.

Now put aside the upper part of the pack.

Please count the remaining cards onto a pile on the table. Put them face-downward, one card at a time.

Now remove the top card and the bottom card.

Here we've reached the tricky bit. Kindly pick up and study the card that is now at the top of the pile. Look at it carefully. Don't let me see it. But think about it. Concentrate hard.

Is your card a black card?

"It is."
Is your card an Ace?
"It is."
Is your card the Ace of Spades?
"It is!"

The secret: Before performing the trick you have checked to see what the next-to-the-bottom card in the pack is. In this case, it was the Ace of Spades. All you have to do now is remember the Ace of Spades.

Your victim begins by cutting the pack in two and discarding the top part. This doesn't change the position of the Ace of Spades. Then he counts out the remaining cards onto a pile on the table, which reverses their order. The Ace of Spades, having begun as the next-to-the bottom card, is now the next-to-the-top card, so that when the top and bottom cards have been removed, the top card has to be the Ace of Spades.

The time you spend in discovering that the card *is* the Ace of Spades is just a lot of showmanship!

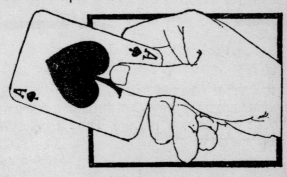

Hole in one

Equipment: 1 nickel
               1 piece of paper with a small
               round hole in it

The trick: Let's get on with the magical challenge! I have here a nickel and a piece of paper. In the middle of the piece of paper is a hole. As you can see, the hole is just about the size of a dime.

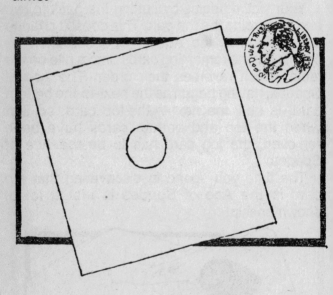

Now what I would like to know is this: can anyone here pass the nickel through the tiny hole without tearing the paper? They can't. Well, watch me do it!

The secret: Unless a member of your audience already knows the secret — which is just possible, but most unlikely — not one of them will be able to pass the nickel through the hole without tearing the paper.

To perform the impossible yourself, you must fold the sheet of paper in two right through the center of the hole and then slide the coin inside the folded paper so that part of it shows through the hole.

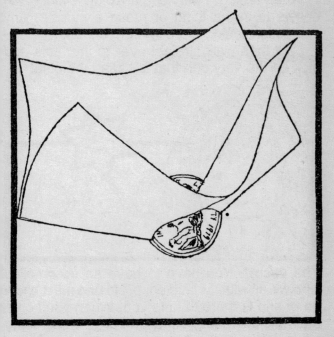

Now pull the paper very gently downward and outward on both sides of the coin and watch how easily the coin slips through the hole.

Hide and seek

Equipment: 3 cups
1 coin

The trick: On my table I have three cups and one coin. I'm going to leave the room and, while I am gone, I would like a member of my audience — any member at all — to step forward and hide the coin under one of the three cups.

When I return I will need absolute silence. No one is to say a thing or move a muscle. Any distraction could disturb my concentration.

I will then walk straight over to the table and pick up the very cup that is hiding the coin!

The secret: You have to have an accomplice who will sit with the audience. No one must know he or she is there to help you. When you come back into the room, your accomplice will be using a finger as a signal. If he or she is holding a finger on the middle of the mouth it means the coin is hidden under the middle cup.

If your accomplice is holding a finger to the left of his or her mouth it means the coin is hidden under the left-hand cup.

If your accomplice is holding a finger to the right of his or her mouth it means the coin is hidden under the right-hand cup.

If your accomplice is holding three fingers on the mouth it means the audience has tried to out-smart you and put coins under all three cups. If the fingers are nowhere near the mouth it means that the audience has tried to out-outsmart you and has not hidden the coins under the cups at all!

The disappearing thimble

Equipment: 1 thimble
1 scarf

The trick: This little object is a thimble. It's a magic thimble. I'm going to cover it with this scarf and make it disappear!

Watch carefully. I'm holding the thimble in my left hand. I cover the thimble and my hand with the scarf. The thimble is still underneath, isn't it? If you don't believe me, you can reach under the scarf and feel it. Please feel under the scarf, sir. And you, madam. And you, sir. And you. And you. It is still there, isn't it?

It's there now, but if I just say the magic word *Shazzam!* and take away the scarf, you'll find the thimble has disappeared!

It's gone — and you can search the scarf, you can search the stage, and you can search me, but I promise you, you won't find that thimble. It's a magic thimble, after all.

The secret: You have an accomplice in the audience. When you are asking the members of the audience to feel under your scarf to make sure the thimble is still there, your accomplice, the last person to whom you offer your hand, takes the thimble away!

The audience really can search the scarf, the stage, and you, and they won't find that thimble because your secret accomplice has slipped it into a pocket.

Coins in the hat

Equipment: 10 dimes, each one dated
a different year
1 hat
1 blindfold

The trick: I would like a member of the audience to step forward and assist me with this trick. Thank you, madam. Would you please begin by blindfolding me. Make quite sure that I can't see a thing.

Now you will see that on the table I have arranged ten coins. They are all dimes and each one belongs to a different year. What I would like you to do is to choose one coin. Now take that coin and pass it around the audience. Get everyone to look at it closely and memorize the date carefully.

Now bring the coin back to the table and put it and all the other coins into my top hat. Shake the hat a little so that the coins are all jumbled up. Now pass me the hat, but hold it up high. I will feel inside the hat and find your coin.

Here it is!

The secret: Before you perform this trick place all ten coins in the freezer compartment of a refrigerator. This will make them very cold, and they will stay cold even if you bring them into a warm room and don't use them right at the beginning of your performance.

The coin that the member of the audience

chooses from the ten will be passed around and handled by lots of different people. Their handling of it will make it a lot warmer than the other nine coins, so that when you put your hand inside the hat all you have to do is feel each coin until you come to one that's warmer than the others. That's the coin you want. Now produce it from the hat and tell the audience its date.

Shapes shake-up

Equipment: 1 sheet of writing paper
1 pencil
1 hat
1 blindfold

The trick: I'm wearing a thick blindfold. I can't see a thing, and yet when I ask members of my audience to draw shapes onto slips of paper for me I will be able to tell them the shapes they have drawn! It sounds impossible. It *is* impossible. But I can do it!

Let me tear a piece off this sheet of writing paper and give it to a member of the audience. Now, sir, would you kindly draw a triangle onto your piece of paper, fold the paper in two, and place it inside my top hat.

Let me tear off another piece of writing paper and give it to someone else. Now, madam, would you kindly draw a circle onto the paper, fold it, and place it inside that hat.

Finally, let me give this last bit of paper to a

third member of the audience. Now, sir, would you be so kind as to draw a square onto the paper, fold the paper, and place it inside that hat.

Now all three folded pieces of paper are inside that hat. Would someone kindly hold the hat up so that all can see it? I will now pick out one of the pieces of paper and tell you what shape is drawn on it, even though I am totally blindfolded...It's the CIRCLE!

The secret: It's so simple, you'll be surprised when you hear how it's done! The first and third pieces of paper you tore off will both have one rough torn edge and three smooth edges. But the second piece will have *two* rough torn edges and two smooth edges.

Since you know that the circle was drawn on the second slip of paper and you also know that the second slip of paper has two rough edges, all you have to do is feel all three slips of paper inside the hat and pick out the one with two rough edges.

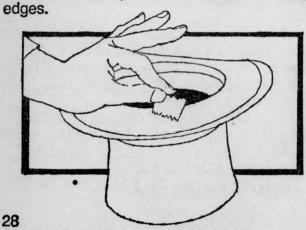

The rattling matchbox

Equipment: 4 matchboxes
               1 coin

The trick: As you can see, I have here three empty matchboxes. Would somebody from the audience kindly inspect the matchboxes.

Now, sir, will you be so good as to lend me a coin. Thank you. Place the coin in one of the three matchboxes. Close all three matchboxes and line them up for me on the table.

Watch me while I shuffle the three matchboxes. Your coin is in this box isn't it? Yes, I can hear it rattling. Now let me shuffle them again. Can you find the matchbox containing the coin?

You're wrong! Your coin's in this one.

The secret: You a have fourth matchbox hidden up your sleeve! You keep it in place with a rubber band just above your wrist. The hidden matchbox also contains a coin.

When you shuffle the three matchboxes the first time, you deliberately pick up a matchbox you know to be empty and give it a shake. Although it is empty, the matchbox up your sleeve will rattle and your audience will think it is the matchbox you are holding that is rattling. This will fool the member of the audience who has got to choose the box containing the coin, so that when you shuffle all three boxes a second time, he is almost certain to pick up the empty box that he thought he heard rattling.

The nine-card trick

Equipment: 9 cards

The trick: I'm going to lay nine cards out on the table, face-upward like this.

Now I'm going to leave the room. While I'm out of the room I want you to choose one of the nine cards. When I return I will ask one of you to point to each of the cards in turn, and when that person points to the card you have chosen I will tell you.

The secret: When you come back into the room after the secret card has been chosen, the member of the audience who points to the cards is actually your accomplice. He or she will touch each card in a particular place and the place that is touched will indicate the secret card's position on the table. So if your accomplice touches all the cards in the top left-hand corner, you will know that the secret card is the one in the top left-hand corner of the lay-out, and if each card is touched right in the middle, you will know the card you want is in the center.

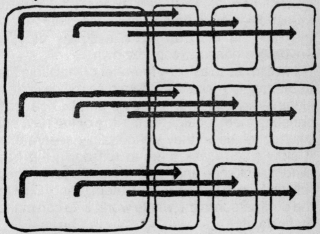

To make the trick a bit more baffling, you can arrange for your accomplice to touch the card in the position you need to know just once. If your accomplice shows you where the secret card is when pointing to the first card, all the other cards can be touched in different places and help to confuse the audience.

The dancing dice

Equipment: 2 dice
1 tray

The trick: Don't ask me why,
But just one dice is called a *die*.
What's more, I have it on the best advice,
You must have *two* to call them *dice!*

You see, I'm not just a great magician — I'm a brilliant poet as well! And all that's by way of introducing you to these two very ordinary-looking dice. In fact, they are ordinary dice in anybody's hands except my own.

I would like to ask any member of the audience to attempt to make these two dice roll down this sloping tray without coming apart. You can squeeze them together at the top of the tray, but as they roll down they will certainly separate.

Now when *I* ask them to roll down the tray clinging onto one another, they do as I ask. They roll from top to bottom without separating. But I'm the only person in the whole world who can make them do it!

The secret: The secret lies on the tip of your tongue! When you give the two dice to any member of the audience who wants to try to roll them down the sloping tray without separating, the dice are quite dry. But before you roll them down the sloping tray yourself, you moisten one

side of each of the dice with a little saliva and stick the two dice together at an angle. The dice will now run down the sloping tray without coming apart.

Don't actually lick the dice or your audience will guess what you are up to! Pretend to cough, and as you put your hand to your mouth, lick a couple of your fingers. Then transfer the saliva from your fingers to the sides of the dice.

Explosive!

Equipment: 1 paper bag
1 dollar bill
4 quarters

The trick: Ladies and gentlemen, I have here one slightly crumpled brown paper bag. As you can see, it's completely empty.

Now I would be grateful if a member of the audience would be kind enough to give me a dollar bill. I say *give* and not *lend*, because you may never see it again! But don't worry — if I make your dollar disappear, I'll give you four quarters to make up for it.

Thank you very much, madam. Now watch carefully while I fold up your dollar and pop it into the paper bag. I will now blow up the paper bag — and burst it. BANG! I'm afraid your dollar has disappeared, but I think I can find four quarters for you. With a bit of magic, I should be able to produce them for you. Where would you like them to be — in my shoes, in my pockets, inside my hat? In my shoes? Very well, let me remove my shoes — and here are your quarters!

The secret: Your ordinary brown paper bag isn't ordinary at all! It contains a secret pocket, made of the same crumpled brown paper and glued to the inside of the bag.

When you show your audience that the bag is empty all you do is turn it upside down and shake it. Nothing will fall out. You then place the folded dollar bill inside the bag's secret pocket instead of inside the bag itself. When you blow up the whole bag and burst it, the dollar won't fall out because it is safely hidden away in the secret pocket. You immediately crumple up the bag and throw it away (only to rescue it and the hidden dollar after the show, of course!) while you distract your audience by talking about the quarters and asking them where they would like them to appear.

Before performing the trick you will have hidden four quarters in your shoes, and in your pockets *and* in your hat, so that whichever place is chosen will have the quarters ready and waiting!

Paperback power

Equipment: 1 paperback book
               13 coins

The trick: In my hand I am holding one of the great works of world literature. It's an amazing book — how amazing you'll discover.

For this trick, I need the assistance of a member of the audience. Thank you, madam.

Would you please pick up the ten coins that are on the table and count them. There really are just ten there, aren't there? Good. Now please place the ten coins on top of the cover of the book. That's right.

Now please cup your hands and watch me while I tip all the coins from the top of the paperback into your hands.

You've got the ten coins. Let me give you another one. I know you can't see it, but it's there all right. And here's another. And here's a third invisible coin — all three of them plucked from thin air!

You should find you are now holding thirteen coins. You don't believe it? Count them out and you'll see I'm right.

The secret: Before beginning the trick, hide three extra coins inside the front cover of the book. Put them in the center of the inside of the front cover, so that when you flick through the pages of the book no one will notice them.

Once your volunteer from the audience has counted out the ten coins on top of the cover, you then tip them into her cupped hands. As you tip the book up, the three coins hidden inside the cover will fall out as well. If you tip the book sharply, the extra three won't be noticed as they fall into her hands.

You then pretend to pluck three invisible coins out of thin air and throw them into her cupped hands. When she counts out the coins at the end of the trick, she will find she really does have thirteen there — to her surprise and your delight!

Change the Ace

Equipment: 3 cards

The trick: As you can see I have here three Aces: the Ace of Spades, the Ace of Diamonds, and the Ace of Clubs.

With your help I can change one of these Aces. Let me gather the three cards up, turn them over, and invite a member of the audience to blow on them. Well done!

Now I've got the Ace of Spades, the Ace of Clubs, and the *Ace of Hearts*!

The secret: The secret lies in the fact that you had the Ace of Hearts on you all the time! When you held up the three Aces at the beginning of the trick, you said the middle Ace was the Ace of Diamonds and your audience believed you because it looked like the Ace of Diamonds. If you hold the Ace of Spades and the Ace of Clubs, over the Ace of Hearts so that only the pointed part of the heart shows, the card will be mistaken for the Ace of Diamonds.

At the end of the trick you simply reveal the three cards to be what they are: the Ace of Spades, the Ace of Clubs and the Ace of Hearts.

This is a very simple trick, bit if it is performed quickly it will fool your audience. It is an excellent trick to use right at the beginning of a routine of several card tricks.

Two-star tricks

The magic bracelet

Equipment: 1 piece of string
                1 bracelet

The trick: I need two members of the audience to come up and assist me please.

Now what I would like you to do is to tie one end of this piece of string to my left wrist and the other end of the piece of string to my right wrist. Tie the string with as many knots as you like.

Here I have a simple bracelet. I would be grateful if you would inspect it. Thank you. Now hand it to me and kindly return to your seats.

I will now turn my back on you for ten seconds — and when I turn around again you will find that the bracelet has been threaded onto the string!

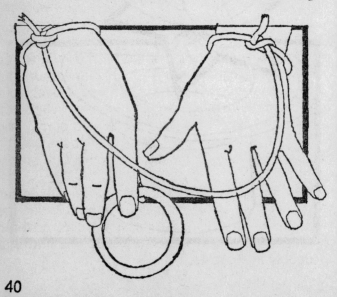

The secret: There's a second bracelet — identical to the first — and you've had it hidden up your sleeve all the time!

When you come on to perform this trick you have already hidden the secret bracelet up one of your sleeves. You have pushed it over your wrist and wedged it up your sleeve. When you turn your back on the audience you simply slip the bracelet they have seen into a pocket, reach up your sleeve, and pull down the secret bracelet!

When you have practiced this trick a few times you will feel confident enough to do it facing the audience with your hands and wrists covered with a black cloth. The audience will find that doubly impressive.

The mighty mind reader

Equipment: Several slips of paper
A few pencils
1 hat

The trick: Ladies and gentlemen, here are some blank slips of paper. I would like to give a slip to each of you.

Now would you be so kind as to write a two, three, or four word message on your slip of paper. The message can be about anything you like. When you have written your message, fold up the piece of paper so that no one can see what you have written. Now place your folded slips of paper inside my hat.

I will now proceed to amaze you with the mightiest example of mind reading you have ever witnessed. I will pick out a slip of paper, hold it to my forehead and tell you what is written on the slip of paper. I will do it with every folded paper in turn. When I have finished I would like any member of the audience whose message I have not read out to stand up. I guarantee that not one of you will stand up!

The secret: Before beginning this trick you have written a two, three, or four word message of your own on an extra slip of paper and hidden it inside the hat, tucked somewhere along the lining where no one will see it.

When you pick out the first slip of folded paper from the hat and press it to your forehead, you read out the message you have written on your hidden slip. You then open the slip you held to your forehead as if you are checking it, but in fact you are reading what your *next* message is going to be.

Working this way, each time you hold a slip of paper to your forehead the message you read out is, in fact, the message you read on the last piece of paper you looked at.

When you get to the last of the real messages, remove your own hidden slip of paper and hold it to your forehead while you announce the final message that was written by a member of the audience. You will then have told everyone their messages without appearing to have read any of them!

For this trick to be truly effective you need an audience of a least fifteen people. With fewer people, someone may notice that you announced one more message than there are members of the audience.

String so strong

Equipment: 1 piece of string
1 straw
1 pair of scissors

The trick: I have here a perfectly ordinary piece of string. Would you care to inspect it, madam?

And I have here a perfectly ordinary drinking straw. Now I will thread the string through the straw so that there is a piece of string hanging out of both ends of the straw.

Now I will bend the straw with the string in it and cut the string and the straw in two — like so!

You saw me cut it, didn't you? Now watch me blow on it.

I've blown on it, and I've mended it! Madam, would you please pull the string out of the straw and check that it is still in one piece just as it was when your first inspected it. The string is in one piece, but the straw is cut in two!

The secret: The secret lies in the straw, which you did *not* offer for inspection.

Before performing the trick you should make a neat cut about an inch long in the middle of the straw, so that when the straw is bent, with the cut on the inside, the string, if the ends are pulled, will come clear of the bend. You keep the exposed stretch of string hidden from the audience with your thumb and forefinger while you cut through the straw with the scissors.

Finally you hold the pieces of straw in your closed hand while you invite a member of the audience to pull the complete piece of string out of the straw. While the member of the audience is holding up the piece of string, you hold up the two pieces of straw and the rest of the audience bursts into thunderous applause!

Red, white and blue

Equipment: 6 silks — two red, two white, and two blue

The trick: On my table I have three very attractive and very remarkable silk handkerchiefs: one red, one white, and one blue. In my pockets I have nothing at all — as you can see.

I am going to tie the red handkerchief to the blue handkerchief like this, and place them in my right-hand pocket. To make sure there's no cheating I'll let you see the end of the blue handkerchief at all times. I'll pull it slightly out of the pocket so you can keep an eye on it.

Now I will put the white handkerchief inside my left-hand pocket. And here comes the magic! I'm now going to send the white handkerchief from my left pocket over to my right pocket — VOOMVOOMVOOM! It's done!

Watch me pull out the blue handkerchief from my right-hand pocket. The white handkerchief is tied to it now! Here they are: the red, the white, and the blue all tied together in a row!

The secret: You begin the trick with *six* silks, not three. You have two reds, two whites, and two blues. Before performing the trick, tie one white silk between one red and one blue, roll them into a tight bundle and hide them in the dead corner of your right-hand pants, or slacks, pockets.

When you begin the trick you can show your audience the linings of both your pockets and they will think your pockets are empty. When you have tied the red and blue silks together and are seen to place them in your right-hand pocket, push them right into the pocket so that they are out of sight, saying, "To make sure there's no cheating, I'll let you see the end of the blue handkerchief at all times." You then pull out the blue end of the three handkerchiefs hidden in the dead corner of your pocket. With practice you will be able to do this as though it were all one movement, and your audience won't realize that the corner of blue handkerchief isn't the same handkerchief as the one they saw you put in your pocket.

Once you have put the white silk into your left

pocket you can forget about it, though if you want to show that your left pocket is completely empty when you have shown the three handkerchiefs tied together, you can carefully move the white handkerchief into the left pocket's dead corner while your audience is applauding madly.

Indian rope trick

Equipment: 1 rope
1 bottle
small piece of cork

The trick: The trick I am about to show you is one of the oldest pieces of magic in the world. It has been performed by great Indian magicians for thousands of years.

Here I have a very old Indian medicine bottle, and here I have a short length of Indian rope. Watch me place the rope inside the bottle. Now watch me turn the bottle upside down. Whoops! The rope has fallen out. That's because I forgot to say the ancient Indian magic word. I'll say it now and we'll see what happens. PINDIPINDIDIRIPU!

Look, when I turn the bottle over, the rope stays where it is and — even more amazing — I can swing the bottle by the rope.

Now if you care to examine the bottle and the rope for yourselves, you will see that this trick can only be performed by a true magician.

The secret: Inside the bottle you have hidden a small piece of cork. When you turn the bottle upside down the first time, you are careful not to turn it right upside down. You just turn it enough for the rope to fall out. When you next turn the bottle upside down you do it properly, so that the small piece of cork gets stuck between the neck of the bottle and the rope. Now the rope won't fall out, and you can even swing the bottle with the rope.

When you want to remove the rope from the bottle, turn it the right way up and push the rope down into the bottle. This will allow the cork to drop to the bottom of the bottle. Pass the rope to your audience for them to examine. While they are taking the rope from you, hold the bottle upside down with the mouth of the bottle in your palm. The piece of cork will fall into your hand, and you can then pass the bottle to the audience in safety.

You will need to practice with different sizes of bottle, rope, and cork before you get the trick just as you want it. A medicine bottle, or a bottle of dark-colored glass, is ideal. The width of the rope and the piece of cork together should be slightly greater than the opening of the neck of the bottle.

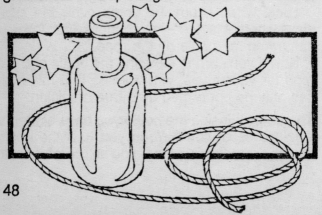

The wand and handkerchief

Equipment: 1 handkerchief
1 wand

The trick: You see here my left fist. Watch me cover it with this handkerchief. Now watch me push the wand into my fist. It's pushing the handkerchief with it, as you can see.

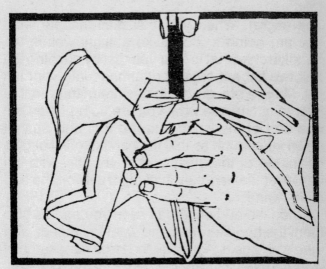

It's a real fist, a solid wand, and a handkerchief without holes. Have a look if you don't believe me.

Now I'm going to push the wand right through the handkerchief, without breaking the wand or tearing the handkerchief! Here goes.

I've done it!

The secret: When you first demonstrate what you are going to do, make a slight well in the handkerchief that is over your fist by pushing the first two fingers of your right hand into your left fist. Make a big, dramatic gesture of this, so that everyone can see what you are doing. Then put one end of the wand into the well and push it down far enough so that the handkerchief begins to appear at the other end of your fist with the center of the handkerchief obviously on the end of the wand.

Once the audience has seen you do this give them the handkerchief and want to inspect, and then start again. Again lay the large handkerchief over your left fist with the center of the handkerchief over the opening, and once more make a grand gesture of creating a small well with the first two fingers of your right hand. This time however, only one of your fingers goes inside your fist, and the other goes outside your left thumb. It is into this "well" that you poke your wand this time and, of course, it slips through without difficulty.

This is a very effective trick, but requires plenty of practice before it can be performed perfectly.

Read the pack!

Equipment: 1 pack of cards
                 1 blindfold

The trick: I am blindfolded. I cannot see with my eyes, but I can see with my incredible magician's mind!

Here I have a pack of cards. I will hold it out so that it faces, you and I will go through the pack telling you the name of each card in turn.

I got all fifty-two of them right, didn't I? And the pack was facing you all the time, and I was blindfolded. Unbelievable — and yet you saw it happen!

The secret: This fantastic trick has you fooling the audience twice. First, you can just see under the bottom of the blindfold. But, more important, the real magic is in the way you present the pack of cards.

Before beginning the trick, hold the pack of cards face downward and turn the top card face upward. When you hold out the pack to face the audience, have this card facing them. They will think, very naturally, that this is actually the bottom card in the pack. As they are looking at the card, you name it for them, at the same time noting the card that is facing you, by peeping under the blindfold.

When you have named the first card, put the pack behind your back and transfer the card you have just glanced at to the "audience" side of the pack. Now show the pack to the audience, naming the card they can now see and noticing the new one that is facing you. Continue this until you have been right through the pack. You will know when you have named all fifty-two cards because all that will face you is the back of a card — the back of the card you first showed your audience.

The trick is amazing enough performed without a blindfold, but the blindfold makes it that extra bit special. It also makes it that bit trickier to perform.

Telepathy

Equipment: None

The trick: I'm going to need an assistant for this trick. Are there any volunteers? You, sir? Thank you very much. If you will step over here, I will explain to you what I would like you to do. Don't worry, it's very simple.

I am going to leave the room and, while I am out of the room, I want the rest of the audience to choose an object in the room. When I return I want you to name various objects in the room and when you have named the one the audience has chosen, I'll tell you. Okay?

(Five minutes later)

Well, here I am again. Has the audience chosen an object?

"They have."

Good. Now start giving me some ideas.

"Is it the fireplace?"

No.

"Is it the clock?"

No.

"Is it the picture?"

No.

"Is it the table?"

No.

"Is it the doorknob?"

Yes it is!

The secret: The assistant you invite to join you from the audience is, in fact, your accomplice. When your accomplice is asking you what you think the object is, just before the right object is mentioned, an object that has four legs will be mentioned. As soon as your accomplice has mentioned an object with four legs, by asking, "Is it a chair?" or "Is it a table?" or "Is it the cat?" you know that the next object *must* be the one you're looking for. It will always be.

You can repeat this trick many times before the rest of the audience begins to suspect what's up, but it's probably best not to try it more than three times at the same performance.

Touch a card

Equipment: 1 pack of cards

The trick: I need several members of the audience to come and help me with this trick. Please step forward and stand around my table.

Now I have an ordinary pack of cards here that I would like one of you to shuffle for me. Thank you. I'm now going to lay these cards out on the table face downward and in no particular order.

Now I would like each one of you in turn to touch a card. Yours, sir, is the Queen of Spades. Let me see it. Yes, I'm right. And yours, madam, is the Three of Hearts. Right again. And yours, sir, is the Eight of Diamonds. Right once more. And yours is the Six of Spades. Right again, I'm pleased to say. Now I think I'll have a go at touching one myself. I reckon it's the Four of Hearts. And so it is.

Here are the five cards for you to see for yourselves — the Queen of Spades, the Three of Hearts, the Eight of Diamonds, the Six of Spades, and the Four of Hearts!

The secret: After the cards have been shuffled make sure you notice the bottom card of the pack and remember it. In this case it was the Queen of Spades. When laying out the cards on the table you can put them down in any order you like, but be sure to note where the bottom card goes and try to position it where one of your audience is least likely to choose it.

When the three or four members of the audi-

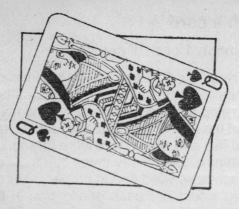

ence have each touched a card, tell the first volunteer that his card is the Queen of Spades. Pick it up, without letting him see it, check it yourself, and make sure that it is indeed the Queen of Spades. It isn't, of course.

Now tell the second volunteer what card she has chosen, naming the card you are now holding in your hand, and pick up the second card as if to check it, again making sure none of the audience sees the card. This second card will be the one you name when your third volunteer is touching his card.

When you have named each of your volunteers' cards, say you are going to touch a card yourself and touch the Queen of Spades, saying, of course, that it is whatever the last card you saw was. If you place the Queen of Spades at the top of the little pile of cards in your hand, you can turn over the five cards in your hand and show your audience that they were indeed the five cards you said they were.

Your number's up!

Equipment: Pencil, paper, and envelope

The trick: I am going to write a number on this piece of paper, fold the piece of paper in two, put it in an envelope, seal the envelope, and place the sealed envelope on the table in full view of the entire audience. I will not touch that envelope again until the end of the trick.

Now I am going to take another piece of paper and write down three numbers that you are going to give me. I'd like someone to tell me their date of birth. In what year were you born, sir?

"1965."

1965. Good. I've written that down. Now under that I'd like to put a famous historical date. Can you suggest one, madam?

"1066."

1066. Fine. That will go under 1965. Now, just to make the trick even trickier, I'm going to ask someone to write down a third number underneath the first two, without telling me what the third number is. Will you do this for me, sir? Thank you. Now pass the paper to someone else and get them to add the three numbers together and tell us what they total.

"4142."

Now if someone else would step forward and open the envelope on the table I think they will find that 4142 is the very number I wrote down at the beginning!

The secret: You have a secret helper in the audience who is the person who writes down the third number for you. Before beginning the trick you have told your accomplice what number you are going to put inside the envelope — it can be any number at all over 4000 — so that your accomplice's job is to write down a number which, when added to the first two numbers called out by real members of the audience, will add up to the number you want.

Your accomplice will have to be good at math and be able to do additions very quickly. As you pass your accomplice the piece of paper with 1965 and 1066 on it, he or she must mentally add those two numbers together (1965 + 1066 = 3031) and then take the answer away from the number 4142 you have written on a piece of paper (4142-3031 = 1111) to get the number 1111 to write down. Then the paper is passed along to someone else to check.

The thimble vanishes

Equipment: 1 thimble

The trick: Now, I'd like to practice throwing thimbles today. I've gotten very good at it — in fact, thimble throwing is my favorite hobby.

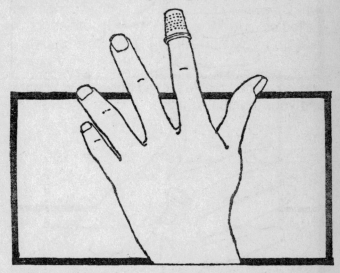

Now madam, if you concentrate very hard, I'll throw the thimble to you. There it goes!

It's no longer on my finger as you can see. In fact, it seems to have disappeared. Could it be flying through the air with the greatest of ease? Yes, I think it is. And I think it's going in your direction madam. Yes, it is. Let me come over to you. Here it is. The thimble you wanted is hiding behind your right ear!

The secret: When you pretend to throw the thimble into the air, you bend your forefinger back like this,

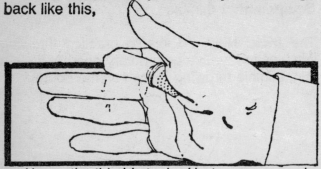

and leave the thimble tucked between your palm and your thumb like this.

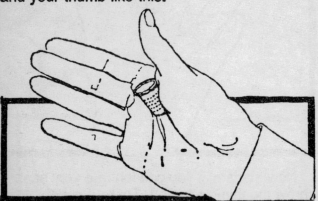

If you do this quickly while seeming to throw the thimble with your whole hand, the audience will follow the "path" of the thimble through the air.

When you go to find the thimble, you simply put your forefinger back into it when your hand is behind the lady's head and produce your finger with the thimble on it.

Three-star tricks

The magic water

Equipment: 1 bottle of water
1 drinking glass
1 handkerchief

The trick: Ladies and gentlemen, I am about to turn the water in this bottle into magic water, water that will obey my every command! Let me say the magic word — WIBBLYWOBBLY-WIBBLYWOO — and it's done!

Now I shall pour some of the magic water into this glass. Now I shall cover the glass of magic water with my handkerchief. And now I shall turn the glass upside down, but I will tell the magic water to stay where it is and not fall out.

Look, I've done it!

Now I am going to tell my glass of water, which is still upside down, to start to bubble and boil. Oh, Magic Water, begin to bubble and boil! Yes, it's beginning to bubble — you can even hear the bubbling!

The secret: When you fill the glass, only pour in enough water to make it three-quarters full. When you have covered the glass with the handkerchief, pick it up with your right hand and with your left hand draw the handkerchief's edges under the bottom of the glass. Hold the bottom of the glass and the handkerchief with your left hand and press down the center of the handkerchief with your right hand until it just (but only just) touches the water. Then, with a sharp twist of the wrist turn the tumbler over. Don't worry — the water *won't* fall out.

Now, still holding the tumbler upside down draw the handkerchief around the glass until it becomes tight and smooth across the rim of the glass. The water will now drop to this level (but no farther) and a vacuum without air will have been created at the bottom of the glass. Gradually, air will seep through the handkerchief and travel through the water to fill the vacuum at the bottom of the glass. This will create the boiling and bubbling noises.

The zany zoo-keeper

Equipment: 4 Aces
                 4 Kings
                 4 Queens
                 4 Jacks

The trick: Once upon a time there was a zany zoo-keeper who had four lions, four tigers, four cheetahs, four leopards, and four empty cages. He decided to put a lion into each cage and, since for the purposes of this trick the lions will be the Aces, I will now put four Aces face-upward on the table.

He decided to put a tiger into each cage as well, so I'll now put a King on top of each of the Aces.

He decided to put a cheetah into each cage, so I'll put a Queen on top of each King.

Finally, he decided to put a leopard inside every cage, which is why I'm putting a Jack on top of each Queen.

Unfortunately, the animals all began to fight, and the zoo-keeper suddenly realized that he should have kept the different kinds of animals apart. Now I'll collect the four piles and invite a member of the audience to cut the pack face-downward. Now I'll deal out the sixteen cards into four piles and when you turn the four piles over you will find that the Aces are all together, the Kings are all together, the Queens are all together, and so are the Jacks!

The secret: This trick is one of the all-time "greats." It can't go wrong. It never fails — so long as you play your part properly. No magic is involved. The trick works automatically, provided you deal and collect the cards in the correct order.

Stage 1 When introducing the animals, remember to line up the four Aces, place the Kings on top of them, the Queens on top of them, and the Jacks on top of them.

Stage 2 When you collect the four piles of cards, hold them face downward and have them cut face downward. When you deal them out into four new piles, deal them face downward and go from left to right.

Extra stage If the trick goes well, you might like to add a little bit extra at the end of the trick, by saying that when the zoo-keeper had put the animals into separate cages he stupidly forgot to lock the cages and all the animals escaped and got muddled up again. At this point gather the four piles in your hand, face-downward, cut them, deal them into four new piles, still face downward, then turn them up and you will find you now have four piles, with an Ace, a King, a Queen, and a Jack in each!

Coining it!

Equipment: 1 coin

The trick: To perform this trick I need the kind assistance of a member of the audience. Would you please step this way, madam?

Now all I'm going to do is to tap you on the shoulder with one hand and produce a coin from your ear with the other. Hey presto! I've done it.

Now I'm going to tap you on one knee and produce a coin from behind your other knee. Hey presto! I've done it again.

This time I'm going to tap you on the foot and produce a coin from the back of your neck. Hey presto! I've done it once more!

The secret: The secret of this trick — and of any other trick in which you produce a coin from nowhere — is knowing how to *palm* a coin.

Begin by pressing a small coin into the palm of your hand. Press it in really hard. Now lower the

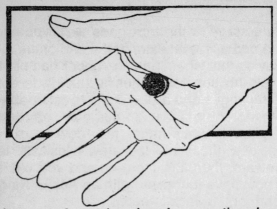

fleshy part of your hand under your thumb over the edge of the coin and try holding the coin in position. At first it won't be easy, but with constant practice you should be able to hold the coin in your palm without difficulty.

When holding a coin in the palm of your hand, don't hold your hand open stiffly because it will then be obvious to the audience that it is not in a natural position. Hold your hand slightly closed and, while the coin is hidden in your palm, use the hand quite normally. When you want to produce the coin, simply relax the muscle in your hand and catch the coin in your fingers.

Once you have mastered the art of palming a coin, you can produce it from absolutely anywhere — from an ear, a knee, the back of the neck!

Dollar power

Equipment: 1 dollar bill

The trick: Is there anyone in the audience lucky enough to have a dollar bill?

Ah, good. Would you hold up the dollar, sir, so that everybody can see it?

Now crumple the dollar into a tiny little ball and kindly throw it to me. Thank you.

Now I shall throw it to another member of the audience. Are you a good catch, madam? You've got it, well done.

Now, madam, would you unfold the dollar and take a close look at the serial number. Would I be right in thinking that the number is A 46737618 A?

I'm right? Well, I'm not surprised!

The secret: You have a second dollar bill already crumpled up and hidden in your palm before the trick begins. You have memorized the serial number of this dollar bill.

Hold the secret dollar bill in your palm. This takes practice, but if you can palm a coin, you should be able to palm a bill as well! When the first member of the audience throws you his bill catch it in both hands, but throw *your* bill to the second member of the audience with one hand, while pocketing the other dollar bill. The audience will be busy watching you throwing the bill and won't notice you putting your hand into your pocket if you do it naturally.

The serial number you announce is, of course, the number on the bill you have thrown to the second member of the audience. And to make the trick more convincing, you can pretend to be having a terrible time trying to think of the serial number, struggling to get it right, and making one or two mistakes along the way!

The vanishing coin

Equipment: 1 handkerchief
                 1 small coin

The trick: This handkerchief that I am holding up before your very eyes may look like an ordinary, everyday handkerchief, but believe me it isn't! It is an incredible handkerchief, an amazing handkerchief, a truly remarkable handkerchief with an *appetite!* Yes, this handkerchief eats money!

Is there a gentleman in the audience who will help me show you how extraordinary this handkerchief really is? I need someone to give me a penny. And when I say give, I mean *give* — because the gentleman who gives his penny to me today will never see it again!

Thank you, sir. Most generous of you.

Now watch closely while I position the coin in the middle of the hungry handkerchief. Now I fold

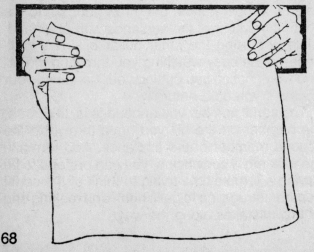

over the corners of the handkerchief like this. The coin is hidden. And if you listen carefully you can hear the handkerchief beginning to eat the coin. Yes, I can certainly hear it: gobble, gobble, gobble it's all gone!

The secret: The secret here lies in a tiny piece of tape (sticky on both sides) that you have hidden in your left hand. When the audience has checked the handkerchief, lay it out on the table and put the coin in the middle. While you are doing this press the little bit of tape onto the left-hand corner of the handkerchief.

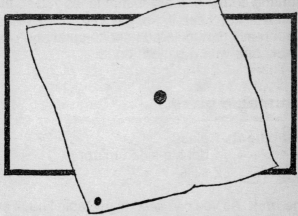

You can keep it hidden with your thumb until you are ready to start folding over the corners of the handkerchief. You begin by covering up the coin with the corner containing the tape and pressing the tape firmly onto the coin. Then cover the coin with the other three corners of handkerchief.

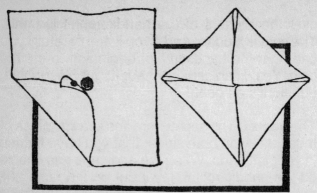

When you hold up the handkerchief at the end of the trick, the coin will be stuck to the bottom left-hand corner of the side that faces you so the audience won't see it. For the trick to work best use a really dark-colored handkerchief and preferably one with a pattern on it.

The magic glass

Equipment: 1 glass
1 double-sided mirror
2 silks

The trick: As you can see, on my table I have an empty glass, and in my hand I have one large silk handkerchief.

Now I am going to cover the empty glass with the handkerchief.

Now I am going to wave my wand over the glass.

Now I am going to remove the handkerchief —

and lo and behold, the glass has been filled with another silk handkerchief!

The secret: It's a trick glass! Down the middle of the glass is a double-sided piece of mirror. The second silk is hidden behind the mirror.

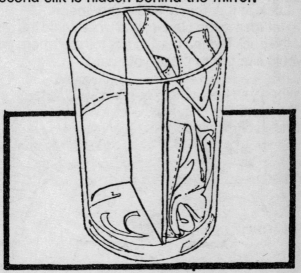

When you first show the glass to the audience, the empty half of the glass is facing them, and because of the mirror, the glass looks totally empty. When you cover the glass with the silk you also turn it around, so that when you uncover the glass the half containing the hidden silk is seen by the audience.

You can easily buy a mirror-glass from any good magic shop. This is one prop that you will not find around your house. And, one of the very few props you might want to buy.

X-ray eyes

Equipment: 1 pack of cards

The trick: I'd like someone to choose a card —
any card — from this pack. Thank you, madam.
 Look at it carefully and remember it.
 Return it to me please, and while I hold the rest
of the pack fanned out like this tell me where you
would like me to place your card.

 In it goes. Now I will close up the pack and look
at it with my amazing X-ray eyes.
 Yes, I think I can see your card now. It was a
red card. It was a Nine. It was the Nine of Hearts!

The secret: Before performing this trick you
need to tamper with one of the cards. Find a

small square of silver paper, or aluminum foil, and paste it to the top left-hand corner of the back of any card.

Have this card as the second card from the top in the pack. When you offer the pack to your volunteer in the audience make sure she doesn't choose your special card!

When your volunteer has chosen her card, studied it and returned it to you, hold the rest of the pack in front of you at the height of your eyes and gently spread the cards out in a fan in your left hand. Hold the chosen card in your right hand and slide it from left to right just above and behind the rest of the pack, asking her to tell you where she would like the card placed. As you do this, you will be able to tell what the card is because you will see its reflection in the foil. Remember that the reflection will be in reverse and, because it will be of one of the card's bottom corners, it will be upside down — so a 6 will look like a 9 and vice versa!

The incredible coin

Equipment: 2 coins
1 glass
1 plate
2 envelopes
1 wand
1 bar of soap

The trick: As you can see, on my table here I have an empty glass on top of which I have balanced an ordinary plate.

Now watch closely, because here I have an extraordinary coin, which I am about to place inside this small brown envelope.

Now I will place the envelope containing the coin on top of the plate and tap the envelope with my magic wand. Hey presto! The coin has gone through the envelope, through the plate, and fallen into the empty glass, so that you can see the coin for yourselves.

The secret: To prepare for this this trick you will need some special secret equipment: a second coin (exactly like the first) and a bar of soap.

The plate already has the second coin stuck onto its underside. You can fix the coin in place by using a little bit of soap. When you tap the plate with your wand, it will shake loose the second coin which will fall into the glass.

If you are very clever, and don't mind practicing the the sleight of hand involved, when you say you are putting the coin into the envelope at the start of the trick you can try slipping it into your lap instead. That way, when the second coin has fallen into the glass you can tear open the envelope and show that the coin is no longer there. Slipping the coin into your lap will only work, of course, if you are sitting behind your table and your audience is directly opposite you.

You could also begin the trick by inviting a member of your audience to place the coin inside the envelope and seal it. Then, at the end of the trick, while members of the audience are inspecting the glass with the second coin in it, slip the sealed envelope into your pocket, at the same time removing a sealed envelope that is empty but looks exactly the same. Pass this empty envelope to a member of the audience and ask that person to open it for you and tell the rest of the audience that it is *really* empty.

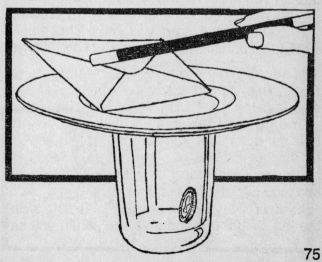

Meet my amazing assistant!

Equipment: 1 pack of cards
                     1 blindfold

The trick: Ladies and gentlemen, I would like you all to meet my amazing assistant. My assistant has the most extraordinary magical powers, as I shall now demonstrate to you.

First of all, I would like a member of the audience to come up on stage and inspect this pack of cards. Would you go through the pack please and remove all the cards of a value less than seven? Thank you. Now would you tie the blindfold around my assistant's eyes? Make sure my assistant cannot see. And make doubly sure by turning my assistant's face away from us.

There are now thirty-two cards left in the pack. Would you pick one out for me? Thank you.

You will agree there is no way my assistant could know what card you have chosen. My assistant certainly can't see it. But I promise you

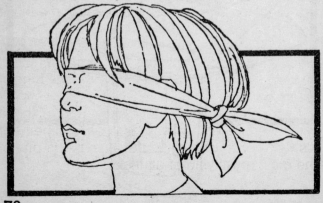

that this amazing assistant of mine will now tell us what the card is.

Now, O amazing assistant, clear your mind. Try to picture the card I'm holding in my hand. Good. Tell me what it is.

"The King of Hearts!"

The secret: You have a code, known only by you and your amazing assistant, and by using the code you can tell him or her exactly what card you are holding, without anybody realizing it. It's a very clever code, difficult to remember and almost impossible to crack. Here it is:

"Now" means it must be a red card. "Really concentrate" means it must be a black card. "Clear your mind" means it's either Hearts or Clubs. "This isn't easy" means it's either Diamonds or Spades. "Picture the card" means it's either an Ace, a King, a Queen, or a Jack. "Is it coming?" means it's either a Ten, a Nine, an Eight, or a Seven. "Fine" means it must be the Ten or the Ace. "Good" means it must be the Nine or the King. "Excellent" means it must be the Eight or the Queen. "Splendid" means it must be the Seven or the Jack.

So that when you say to your assistant, "Now, clear your mind . . . picture the card . . . Good" he knows immediately that the card is the King of Hearts.

Learning the code isn't easy and using it without sounding awkward isn't easy either, but it's well worth working at, because this is one of the most mystifying of all tricks.

A glass with class

Equipment: 1 wine glass
1 large coin (or tiddlywink)
1 small coin (or tiddlywink)

The trick: I take a tall-stemmed glass.

First, I drop a small coin into the glass, and then I

drop in a larger one, like this.

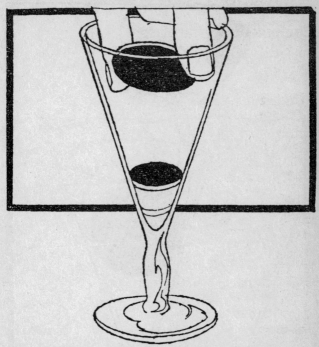

And now I challenge any member of my audience to come and remove the smaller coin from inside the glass, without touching the glass itself or either of the coins.

You can't do it — but I can. Watch!

The secret: All you have to do to perform this little miracle is blow sharply against the edge of the top coin just where it touches the side of the glass. The air will upend the top coin and send the bottom coin shooting out of the glass!

You will probably find the trick easier if you use a larger and smaller tiddlywink instead of two coins. The plastic is lighter than the metal.

With practice you will be able to blow onto the top coin, or tiddlywink, so quickly that no one will even notice. They will think the smaller coin, or tiddlywink, just jumped out of the glass by magic!

The 22-card trick

Equipment: 22 cards

The trick: I've got twenty-two cards here and I'm going to lay them out in three piles on the table face upward. As I'm dealing out the cards I'd like a member of the audience to step forward, choose a card, and remember it. Thank you, madam.

I've dealt the twenty-two cards into three piles for the first time and you've chosen your card. Which pile is it in? That one. Very good.

Now I'm going to gather the cards and deal them into three more piles. Which pile is your card in this time? That one. Fine.

Now I'm going to gather the cards up again and deal them into three piles for the third, and last, time. Which pile is your card in now? That one. Excellent.

Madam, I will now find your card for you.

Here it is!

The secret: This is one of those tricks that works like clockwork and can never go wrong — but you must remember the system!

Stage 1 When you deal the cards for the first time you turn the cards up one at a time and place them on the table in three piles, working from left to right. You will end up with eight cards in the left-hand pile and seven cards in each of the other piles.

Stage 2 After your volunteer has told you in which of the three piles the card of her choice is to be found, you must gather up the three piles. The pile containing the chosen card must always go in the middle between the other two. Begin by picking up the left-hand pile first and placing it face downward in your hand, put the pile containing the chosen card on top of the left-hand pile and the remaining pile on top of that. Always begin by picking up the left-hand pile, unless it is the left-hand pile which contains the chosen card. In that case it does not matter which pile you pick up first, as long as the left-hand pile goes in the middle between the other two.

The cards are dealt into three piles and collected in this way, three times in all.

Stage 3 When you have collected the three piles in the correct order for the last time, start turning up the cards in the pack from the top, one by one. The chosen card will be the *eleventh card* in the pack *every* time.

The great escape

Equipment: 2 pieces of rope, each about a yard long

The trick: I would like a member of the audience to come on stage please and tie me and my assistant together. Please begin by tying the ends of one rope to my wrists. Now loop the second rope around my rope and tie the ends of it to my assistant's wrists.

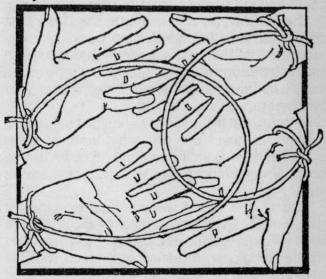

You will agree that we are tied together now, that there is no way we can escape from each other without untying the knots or cutting the rope. That's what you think! But we are two of the world's greatest magic masters, so that before we've had time to say A NOD'S AS GOOD AS A WINK TO A BLIND HORSE* we've escaped.

The secret: You and your assistant will have to practice this trick time and again before you can master it. If you can do it, it will amaze your audience, but you will have to work hard at it because it isn't easy.

To escape, this is what you must do: with your right hand grasp the loop of the rope that's tied to your assistant's wrists. Bring this loop to the inside of your left wrist, tuck it right under the rope that's tied there, and push it into the palm of your left hand. Now, without twisting it, pass it over the fingers of your left hand, step back, and you should be free! If you have remembered to push the loop through from the back of the rope round your wrist and have drawn it forward over your left fingers, you *will* be free.

In order that the audience shouldn't see exactly what is going on, you must work at great speed and wave your arms up and down as you do it. Entertaining patter will distract them as well.

This is one of the world's most spectacular magic tricks. Even professional magicians find it hard work. Houdini, the great showman and master magician, mystified audiences with his escape tricks. If you can master The Great Escape, you can consider yourself one of the real professionals!

*You repeat this bit of nonsense at least twice, and maybe three times.

Houdini

P.S. A challenge to keep up your sleeve

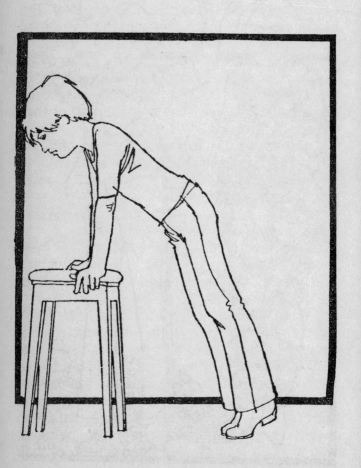

SO YOU THINK YOU'RE SMART, DO YOU?

In every audience you will come across some loud-mouthed know-it-all, who tells everyone that they know exactly how all your tricks are done — and can do several that are a lot better!

Don't worry. That person is no doubt a liar. The more noise they make, the less the rest of the audience will like *them,* and the more the audience will like *you.* However, if they make a real nuisance of themselves, and call out show-stopping remarks like, "That trick's *so easy*!" you will have to deal with them somehow, or they may spoil the show.

The best way is to invite them up onto the stage and say, "If you think you're so smart, I've got a small challenge for you. Since you know so much about magic, I'm sure you will find this very easy, but just to encourage you a bit I will give you a dollar if you can do what I ask!"

Now place a stool against a wall and ask them to face it, standing with their feet together and their toes at a distance about twice the width of the stool away from the wall.

Tell them to bend forward and take hold of both sides of the stool while resting their head against the wall. Now ask them to lift the stool off the floor and stand upright. They simply won't be able to do it! However much you tease and taunt, however much money you offer, they will find it quite impossible — and you can be sure that when they have given up they will return to their seat with a much less swollen head on top of their shoulders!

The Greatest Magic Show on Earth

Once you have practiced all your tricks and mastered all your patter, you will be ready to present The Greatest Magic Show on Earth! Of course, it will only be the *greatest* if you really have perfected your performance with a lot of practice and planned your program with special care.

Always start your show with one of your best tricks and make sure it is one of the ones you feel most confident doing. Always end your show with your most effective and impressive trick. In the middle, perform a number of tricks that show off your skills as a magician. Give the show plenty of variety, be sure to keep it moving, and don't let it go on too long. Don't let your audience get restless and bored. Give them a short show they'll remember and leave them wanting more.

Fifteen minutes is quite long enough for your magic show to last, which means that you will have time to perform seven or eight tricks. In time, you will want to work out a special program for yourself, but to give you an idea of the sort of variety a good magic show needs, here are three different programs, any one of which will give you an exciting quarter-of-an-hour of first class entertainment.

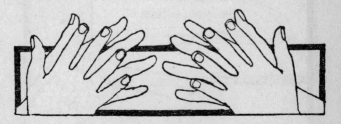

Suggested Program 1
The magic bracelet 40
Red, white, and blue 45
Touch a card 55
A glass with class 78
X-ray eyes 72
Paperback power 35
Shapes shake-up 27
Telepathy 53

Suggested Program 2
Coins in the hat 26
Touch a card 55
The incredible coin 74
Indian rope trick 47
The mighty mind reader 42
Your number's up! 57
The rattling matchbox 29
The great escape 83

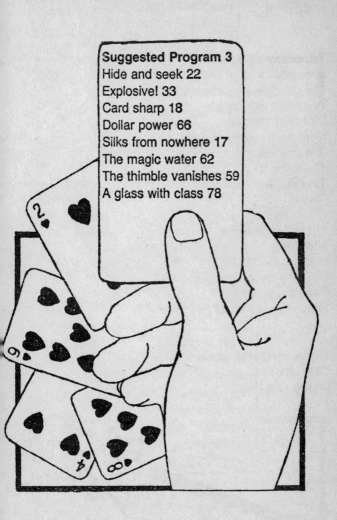

Suggested Program 3
Hide and seek 22
Explosive! 33
Card sharp 18
Dollar power 66
Silks from nowhere 17
The magic water 62
The thimble vanishes 59
A glass with class 78

Index

**Tricks involving coins
and notes**

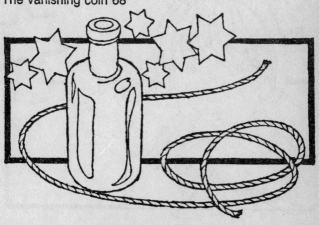

Tricks involving
string and rope

Tricks involving more
unusual props: bracelets
dice, and thimbles

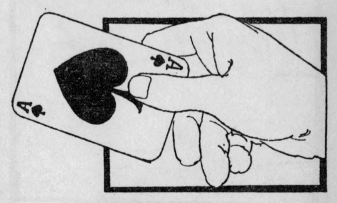